CW01497023

How to Play the Fiddle for Beginners

The Ultimate Guide to Learning, Playing, and Becoming Proficient at the Instrument

Table of Contents

Introduction

In the enchanting world of the fiddle, melodies dance, and emotions sing. If you've ever dreamt of plucking or bowing the strings of this remarkable instrument, then *"How to Play the Fiddle for Beginners"* is your passport to a musical adventure like no other.

This book will empower you to play the fiddle confidently and joyfully, even if you've never picked up a bow. What sets this book apart from other guides on the market is its unwavering commitment to simplicity and hands-on learning. You won't find complex jargon or overwhelming theories here. Instead, you'll discover a gentle, step-by-step approach that gradually builds your skills.

Theory alone won't make you a fiddler. This book is full of practical exercises and techniques you can implement instantly. From proper bowing to tuning your fiddle, every aspect is covered in a way that makes learning enjoyable and effective. You'll find explanations that are easy to follow, ensuring you grasp the concepts and techniques effortlessly.

Playing the fiddle isn't just about notes and strings. It's about expressing yourself through the language of music. This book teaches you how to play and connect with your instrument on a deeper level, allowing you to create stunning melodies that resonate with your soul.

So, if you're ready to embark on a musical journey that's simple, powerful, and utterly enjoyable, *"How to Play the Fiddle for Beginners"* is your key. Whether you've always wanted to play or are just curious about the world of fiddling, this book invites you to discover the joy of making music. Turn the page and let the adventure begin!

Chapter 1: Background to the Fiddle

From ancient folk melodies to modern compositions, the fiddle's sound has resonated through the ages, shaping the essence of musical heritage.

1. *The fiddle's sound has resonated through the ages, shaping the essence of musical heritage. Source:*
https://unsplash.com/photos/man-playing-violin-during-daytime-IsKijub-qHM

In the captivating world of the fiddle, history, culture, and music converge in a symphony of sound and story. In this first chapter, you'll uncover the background of this enchanting instrument, revealing its past and profound impact on countless musical traditions.

This chapter explores the fiddle's versatile role in various music genres. You'll unravel how this instrument transcends boundaries, seamlessly fitting into classical, folk, country, and more, adding a unique sound to each. For those setting out on their fiddling adventure, fear not. This chapter will guide you, setting clear expectations for beginners and illuminating the path ahead. So, grab your bow and prepare to be entranced by the world of the fiddle.

Historical and Cultural Significance

In the vibrant landscape of musical instruments, few hold the same historical and cultural significance as the fiddle. With its roots tracing back centuries, the fiddle has created melodies that transcend time and borders.

The Ancient Origins

The story of the fiddle begins in the mists of antiquity. Its origins are traced to various ancient stringed instruments, like the lyre, played across different civilizations. However, the emergence of the bowed instrument originated in Central Asia and came to Europe during the 9th century, paving the way for the modern fiddle known today.

The early fiddles were simple in design, consisting of just a few strings and a curved bow. While basic in construction, these humble instruments possessed an enchanting quality that resonated with people from all walks of life. They were not merely tools for entertainment but also played a crucial role in religious rituals, celebrations, and storytelling.

The Fiddle in Different Cultures

As the fiddle evolved, it transcended geographical boundaries and cultural divides, becoming a universal instrument with many regional variations. It became the heart of traditional Celtic music in Ireland, producing hauntingly beautiful airs and lively jigs that have stood the test of time.

In the United States, the fiddle took on a distinct sound, fusing with African rhythms to create what is now known as bluegrass and country music. Pioneers like Bill Monroe and Johnny Cash used the fiddle to capture the essence of rural America, creating music that spoke to the soul of a nation.

In Eastern Europe, the fiddle found a home in klezmer music, infusing Jewish celebrations with spirited melodies. In India, it became an integral part of classical music, blending seamlessly with the sitar and tabla to create intricate ragas.

Cultural Significance

The fiddle has been a symbol of joy and sorrow, a companion in times of celebration, and provides solace in times of grief. In Appalachian communities, the fiddle served as a means of expression for the people of the mountains. It was through this instrument that they told stories of their struggles and triumphs, passing down their heritage through generations.

In Ireland, the fiddle is an emblem of national identity. Its mournful strains encapsulate the history of a people who faced centuries of hardship yet preserved their spirit through music. The Irish fiddle has been instrumental in reviving the Irish language and cultural traditions.

The fiddle also plays a pivotal role in classical music. Composers like Antonio Vivaldi and Johann Sebastian Bach incorporated the instrument into their compositions, adding depth and emotion to their masterpieces. The fiddle's versatility allows it to seamlessly transition from rustic folk tunes to the grandeur of the concert hall.

Innovations and Evolution

Throughout history, the fiddle has undergone many innovations. Adding extra strings, fine tuners, and improved materials have enhanced its playability and sound quality. In the modern era, electric fiddles have emerged, taking the instrument to new heights of sonic exploration.

Despite these advancements, the essence of the fiddle remains unchanged. Its ability to convey raw emotion, to tell stories without words, is as potent as ever. Whether it's the mournful wail of a Scottish lament or the frenetic energy of a Texas hoedown, the fiddle can move you in ways that words cannot.

The Fiddle's Enduring Appeal

What is it about the fiddle that gives it such enduring appeal? Perhaps the instrument can bridge the gap between the past and the present. When you listen to a fiddle tune passed down through generations, you are transported to a time when life was simpler yet filled with challenges and joys.

The fiddle also appeals to primal instincts. Its expressive, human-like sound can mimic laughter, tears, and everything in between. When played, it resonates with your emotions, serving as a vessel for your innermost feelings.

Furthermore, the fiddle's accessibility makes it a favorite among musicians and beginners. Its compact size and relatively simple design mean anyone with dedication and practice can play. This inclusivity has allowed the fiddle to remain a beloved instrument across diverse communities.

As you explore its history and cultural significance, you uncover the story of humanity itself. The universal language of music binds us all. So, whether you're a seasoned fiddler or someone who has never picked up a bow, take a moment to appreciate the fiddle's enduring magic and profound impact on this world.

Understanding the Fiddle's Role in Music

The fiddle, with its versatile and dynamic sound, has carved a unique niche for itself in the world of music. While it may be most commonly associated with folk and country genres, the fiddle's role extends beyond these boundaries.

Folk Music: The Fiddle's Home

Folk music and the fiddle are inseparable companions. Across cultures and continents, the fiddle has been an essential element of traditional folk music. In Appalachian communities of the United States, the mournful strains of the fiddle tell stories of hardworking people, their joys, sorrows, and the beauty of their natural surroundings.

2. Folk music and the fiddle are inseparable companions. Source: DTH-BD-NVT, CC BY-SA 4.0 <https://creativecommons.org/licenses/by-sa/4.0>, via Wikimedia Commons: https://commons.wikimedia.org/wiki/File:Cham_monk_with_thei r_traditional_fiddle_in_the_ceremony.jpg

In Irish folk music, the fiddle holds a place of honor, reflecting the Emerald Isle's rich history and cultural heritage. Its lively reels and soul-stirring airs capture the essence of Irish life, from the bustling streets of Dublin to the serene countryside landscapes.

In Scandinavian countries, the fiddle plays a central role in Nordic folk traditions. The haunting melodies of the Hardanger fiddle resonate with the mystique of Nordic forests and fjords, evoking an ancient connection to the land.

Country and Bluegrass: The Heart of America

The fiddle's journey to the United States in the 17th century marked a defining moment in the development of American music. It found a new home in the heartland, becoming an integral part of country and bluegrass.

In country music, the fiddle adds a layer of emotion and storytelling. Think of iconic country songs like Johnny Cash's "Folsom Prison Blues" or Dolly Parton's "Jolene." The fiddle weaves narratives of love, loss, and the American experience into these timeless classics.

Bluegrass music, on the other hand, relies heavily on the fiddle's quick and intricate playing style. Pioneers like Bill Monroe and his Blue Grass Boys introduced the world to the high-energy blend of fiddle, banjo, mandolin, guitar, and bass. The fiddle in bluegrass is like a wild stallion, adding excitement and virtuosity to every performance.

Classical Music: The Fiddle's Elegance

While the fiddle may be more commonly associated with rustic or rural settings, it also shines brilliantly in the refined world of classical music. The violin, as it's known in this context, is a staple of orchestras and chamber ensembles worldwide.

The classical violin repertoire is vast and varied, encompassing everything from the sublime Beethoven and Tchaikovsky to the intricate compositions of Bach and Mozart. The violin's sweet, soaring tones convey a wide range of emotions. The violinist's skill in classical music is often measured by their ability to express the composer's intentions with precision and nuance.

Celtic and World Music: Global Fusion

In Celtic and world music, the fiddle acts as a bridge between different cultures and musical traditions. With Celtic fusion bands like The Corrs, the fiddle adds a contemporary twist to traditional Irish melodies, creating a unique sound that resonates.

In Eastern European and Klezmer music, the fiddle's soulful cries and spirited dances provide a vibrant backdrop to celebrations and gatherings. The klezmer fiddler, with their passionate playing, transforms a wedding or bar mitzvah into an unforgettable musical experience.

Further east, in Indian classical music, the violin has found its place alongside traditional instruments like the sitar and tabla. It brings a Western classical sensibility to India's intricate ragas and rhythms, creating a harmonious fusion of musical worlds.

The fiddle's role in music spans genres and continents, showcasing its remarkable versatility and adaptability. From the rolling hills of Appalachia to the grand concert halls of Europe, the fiddle has left an indelible mark on the musical landscape. As you explore its diverse contributions to folk, country, classical, and world music, you appreciate the fiddle's ability to transcend cultural boundaries and connect people through the universal language of music.

Setting Expectations for Beginners

Learning to play the fiddle is an exciting adventure filled with promise and potential. However, like any musical pursuit, it comes with its own set of challenges and rewards. It's time to set clear expectations for fiddle beginners and help you navigate the path ahead.

1. **The Learning Curve:** Learning to play the fiddle is not an overnight process. It's a journey that requires patience, dedication, and perseverance. The fiddle is notorious for its steep learning curve, especially in the early stages. Don't be discouraged if your first attempts don't resemble the music you admire. Remember,

every fiddler, even the legends, started where you are now.

2. **The Basics Matter:** As a beginner, your first steps should focus on mastering the fundamentals. This includes proper bowing techniques, finger placement on the fingerboard, and learning to read sheet music or tablature. Building a strong foundation in these areas will set you up for success as you progress.

3. **Bowing Techniques:** Bowing is a critical aspect of fiddling. It's what gives the instrument its distinct sound. Learning to control the bow's speed, pressure, and direction is essential for producing beautiful and expressive melodies. Expect to spend a considerable amount of time on bowing exercises and drills.

4. **Scales and Exercises:** Like any other musical instrument, practicing scales and exercises is crucial for developing your skills. These exercises help improve your finger dexterity, intonation, and overall technique. While they may seem repetitive, they are the building blocks of your fiddling journey.

5. **Ear Training:** One of the biggest challenges of the fiddle is its reliance on ear training. Unlike instruments with frets, the fiddle requires you to listen closely to the pitches and nuances of the music you're playing. This skill takes time to develop, so be patient as you work on your ear training.

6. **Repertoire Selection:** Choosing an appropriate repertoire is crucial for a beginner. Start with simple tunes that match your skill level. Irish jigs, folk songs, and basic classical pieces are great options. With time,

confidence, and proficiency, you can gradually tackle more complex compositions.

7. **Frustration and Plateaus:** It's normal to experience frustration and plateaus in your learning journey. There will be moments when you feel stuck and doubt your progress. This is when persistence pays off the most. Push through these challenging phases, and you'll come out the other side as a stronger and more capable fiddler.

8. **Consistent Practice:** Consistency is key when learning to play the fiddle. Regular, focused practice sessions are far more effective than sporadic, lengthy ones. Aim for shorter daily practice sessions rather than marathon practice days. Over time, you'll see steady improvement.

9. **Seek Guidance:** Consider taking lessons from an experienced fiddler or violinist. A teacher can give you valuable feedback, correct your technique, and guide your learning. They can also help you set realistic goals and track your progress.

10. **The Joy of Playing:** While setting goals and working toward them is important, don't forget the primary reason you picked up the fiddle. Embrace the joy of playing, whether a simple folk tune or a more complex classical piece. Music is meant to be a source of inspiration and happiness.

11. **The Journey, Not the Destination:** Remember that learning to play the fiddle is a lifelong journey. There's no rush to become a virtuoso overnight. Embrace each stage of your development, from the early struggles to the breakthrough moments. Your

journey as a fiddler is a story filled with chapters of growth and discovery.

12. **The Fiddle Community:** As you progress on your fiddling journey, consider joining the vibrant community. Attend fiddle festivals, workshops, and local jam sessions. Connecting with other fiddlers can be inspiring and great opportunities for collaboration and learning.

Learning to play the fiddle is a rewarding endeavor that offers a lifetime of musical enjoyment. By setting realistic expectations and understanding the challenges and joys ahead, you'll be better prepared to navigate your fiddling journey. Embrace the process, celebrate your achievements, and let the music you create be a testament to your dedication and passion.

Chapter 2: Getting to Know Your Fiddle

In this journey, it's vital to start with the basics. This begins with getting to know your fiddle inside and out. Your fiddle is composed of the resonating body, the graceful neck, and the soulful strings. Understanding how these elements work together is your first step toward mastering the instrument.

But it's not just about knowing your fiddle. It's also about keeping it in its prime. Proper care and maintenance ensure that your fiddle plays beautifully for years. Your choice of bow and the extras you select also dramatically influence your playing style and tone. This chapter will guide you in selecting the perfect companions for your fiddle.

Anatomy of the Fiddle

To truly master the fiddle, you must begin with a deep understanding of its anatomy. It's time to unravel the intricate components of this enchanting instrument, from the body to the strings that produce its sweet harmonies.

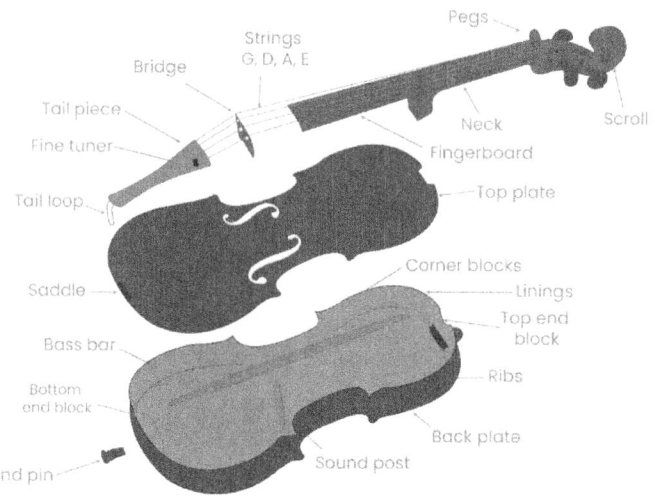

3. To truly master the fiddle, you must begin with a deep
understanding of its anatomy. Source:
*https://www.researchgate.net/publication/304090906/figure/fig4
/AS:548713051705344@1507834794124/Parts-of-a-violin.png*

The Resonating Body: The Heart of the Fiddle

At the heart of every fiddle lies its resonating body, often crafted from fine woods such as spruce or maple. This body is responsible for amplifying the vibrations the strings create, giving the fiddle its unique and enchanting sound.

- **Top Plate (Soundboard):** The top plate, or the soundboard, is a critical component. It's the part that faces upward when you play the fiddle. Its thin, carefully crafted design is what gives the instrument an efficient transmission of sound vibrations, resulting in the fiddle's distinct and resonant tone.

- **Back Plate:** The back plate of the fiddle complements the soundboard by reflecting and enhancing the sound.

Like the soundboard, it's meticulously carved and contributes to the fiddle's acoustic properties.

- **F-Holes:** One of the most recognizable features of a fiddle's body is its f-shaped sound holes, known as F-holes. These meticulously carved openings allow the sound to escape from the resonating body, producing the beautiful and rich tones that define the instrument.

- **Soundpost:** Inside the fiddle, hidden from view, is the soundpost. This small, cylindrical piece of wood connects the top and back plates, playing a crucial role in transmitting sound vibrations and ensuring the instrument's structural integrity.

The Neck and Fingerboard: Where the Magic Happens

The neck of the fiddle is where the player's fingers dance to create melodies. It connects to the body at the top and extends towards the scroll at the headstock.

- **Scroll:** The scroll is a decorative and functional element located at the headstock of the fiddle. Its intricate design adds character to the instrument, while its purpose is to anchor the strings and tuning pegs.

- **Pegbox:** The pegbox is where the tuning pegs are housed. Tuning pegs allow for precise adjustments to the tension of the strings, enabling the player to achieve the desired pitch.

- **Fingerboard:** The fingerboard is a smooth, ebony, or other hardwood surface attached to the neck. It's where the player's fingers press down on the strings to change their length and produce different notes. The careful shaping and positioning of the fingerboard are crucial for accurate intonation.

- **Nut and Bridge:** The nut and bridge are small yet essential components that support the strings and help maintain their height above the fingerboard. The nut is at the top of the fingerboard, while the bridge stands upright between the soundboard and back plate, transmitting vibrations from the strings to the resonating body.

The Strings: The Soul of the Fiddle

The strings are where the magic truly happens in the fiddle. These thin, tightly stretched wires produce the instrument's distinct sounds.

- **Materials:** Fiddle strings are made from steel, synthetic core, or gut. The choice of string material significantly affects the tone and responsiveness of the instrument.

- **Tuning:** The four strings on a fiddle are typically tuned to the notes G, D, A, and E, with G being the lowest and E the highest in pitch. Proper tuning is essential for producing harmonious music.

- **Fine Tuners:** Many fiddles are equipped with fine tuners and small mechanical devices on the tailpiece. Fine tuners allow precise tuning adjustments, especially on the higher-pitched strings (A and E).

- **Rosin:** To create sound, the bow must slide across the strings. Rosin, a resinous substance, is applied to the bow hair to enhance contact, producing clear and resonant tones.

The fiddle stands as a testament to craftsmanship and artistry. Each of its meticulously crafted components, from the resonating body to the strings, plays a vital role in producing the enchanting melodies that have captivated audiences for centuries. As you start your journey to master this captivating instrument, understanding its anatomy will deepen your appreciation and connection to the fiddle's rich history and musical possibilities.

Nurturing the Soul of Your Fiddle: Proper Care and Maintenance

The fiddle, a captivating instrument known for its soulful melodies, demands more than just skilled hands to produce enchanting music. Proper care and maintenance are essential to keep your fiddle sounding beautiful and maintain its longevity.

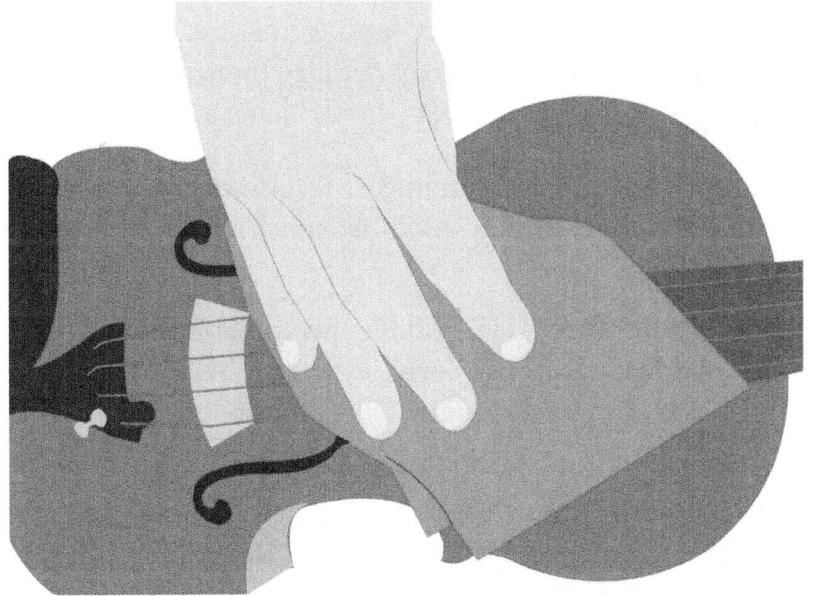

4. Keeping your fiddle clean is paramount. Source: https://www.stradivaristrings.com/wp-content/uploads/2020/11/01-1-3-1.jpg

Cleaning Your Fiddle

Keeping your fiddle clean is paramount. Dust, rosin residue, and even the natural oils from your fingers can accumulate over time and affect the instrument's appearance and sound quality.

- **Soft Cloth:** Use a soft, lint-free cloth to gently wipe down your fiddle after each playing session. This will remove any sweat and rosin buildup. Regularly clean your strings with a separate cloth. Rosin residue accumulates on the strings, diminishing their tone and responsiveness.

- **Fingerboard Care:** If your fingerboard is made of dark wood, occasionally wipe it down with a damp cloth to remove dirt and moisture. Avoid using excessive water, as it can damage the wood.

Humidity Control

Maintaining the right humidity level prevents cracks and warping in your fiddle wood is sensitive to changes in moisture.

- **Humidifier:** Use a fiddle-specific humidifier to keep an ideal humidity level, typically between 40-60%. Place it inside your fiddle case to protect the instrument.

- **Hygrometer:** Invest in a hygrometer to monitor humidity levels inside your case. It will help you make necessary adjustments based on your local climate.

- **Avoid Extremes:** Keep your fiddle away from extreme humidity or dryness, such as radiators and air conditioning vents. Drastic changes can harm the wood.

String Care

Your fiddle's strings are the conduit through which your music flows. Ensuring they're in good condition is crucial for maintaining the instrument's tone and playability.

- **Regular Replacement:** Change your strings regularly, as they lose their brightness and responsiveness over time. Frequency depends on how often you play, but a general guideline is every 6-12 months.

- **Proper Tuning:** Tune your fiddle gently and carefully. Sudden, forceful tuning can put excessive strain on the instrument and its strings.

- **String Lubrication:** Use a small amount of peg compound or chalk on the pegs to ensure they turn smoothly, allowing for precise tuning adjustments.

Bow Maintenance

Your bow is as integral to your fiddle's sound as the instrument. Proper care of the bow ensures it remains supple and responsive.

- **Cleaning the Bow Hair:** Use a soft cloth to gently wipe the bow hair after each playing session. Rosin buildup will affect the bow's ability to grip the strings effectively.

- **Rehairing:** When you notice the bow hair losing its resilience or becoming uneven, it's time for rehairing. A professional luthier can handle this delicate task.

Protecting Your Fiddle During Transport

Whether heading to a gig or simply storing your fiddle, making sure it's protected during transport is crucial.

- **Case Selection:** Invest in a high-quality, well-padded fiddle case that protects against shocks and temperature fluctuations. A hard-shell case is ideal for added safety.

- **Bow Holder:** Many cases have built-in bow holders to keep your bow securely in place during transport.

- **Climate Consideration:** Avoid leaving your fiddle in a hot or cold vehicle for extended periods. Extreme temperatures can damage the instrument.

Storage

When your fiddle isn't in use, proper storage will extend its life and preserve its tonal qualities.

- **Stand vs. Case:** While it's convenient to have your fiddle on a stand for quick access, storing it in its case when it's not in use is better for protection from dust, accidents, and humidity fluctuations.

- **Horizontal Storage:** When storing your fiddle in its case, keep it stored horizontally rather than vertically to prevent undue stress on the neck.

- **Case Humidity Control:** Consider using a case humidifier, especially if you live in an arid climate, to maintain stable humidity levels.

Your fiddle is more than an instrument. It's a companion on your musical journey. Proper care and maintenance are essential to ensure it continues to produce its soul-stirring melodies for years to come. These guidelines will help you preserve your fiddle's beauty and integrity and enhance your playing experience. Remember, your fiddle is a vessel for your musical expression, and nurturing it is an act of love and respect for the music it helps you create.

The Perfect Bow and Accessories

Just as a painter chooses brushes and colors with care, a fiddler must be discerning regarding the bow and accompanying accessories.

The Bow

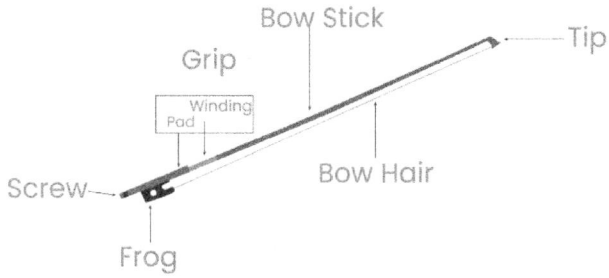

5. A fiddler's connection with their bow is profound. Source: https://musilesson.com/wp-content/uploads/2019/01/Parts-of-the-violin-bow-640x-JPEG.jpg

A fiddler's connection with their bow is profound, and finding the right one is a voyage of discovery. The bow is the conduit through which you express your emotions and create beautiful music.

1. Bow Materials

- **Wood:** Bows are made from various types of wood, with Pernambuco being the most coveted for its balance and resonance. Brazilwood and carbon fiber are also popular choices, offering affordability and durability.

- **Horsehair:** Horsehair is used for the bow's hair. High-quality, unbleached horsehair is preferred for its responsiveness and grip on the strings.

2. Weight and Balance

- **Balance Point:** The balance point of the bow should feel comfortable and natural in your hand. Experiment with different bows to find one that complements your playing style.

- **Weight:** The weight of the bow affects tone and control. Lighter bows are agile and suited for intricate passages, while heavier bows provide power and projection.

3. Bow Length

- **Standard Length:** Most bows are approximately 29 inches long, but variations exist. The right length depends on your arm length.

4. Bow Shape

- **Round vs. Octagonal:** Bows can have a round or octagonal shape. The choice is a matter of personal preference, with some players preferring the octagonal shape for its grip. The octagonal bow is less flexible.

5. Try Before You Buy

- **Test Multiple Bows:** When selecting a bow, try as many as possible. Each bow has a unique personality, and it's essential to find one that resonates with your playing style and preferences.

Essential Accessories

In addition to the bow, several accessories are integral to the fiddler's toolkit. These items not only enhance your playing experience but also protect and maintain your instrument.

1. Rosin

- **Types of Rosin:** Rosin comes in various formulations, each tailored to specific needs. Light rosin is ideal for warm and humid climates, while dark rosin offers better grip in dry conditions.

- **Application:** Apply rosin to the bow hair regularly. A few swipes up and down the bow's hair should suffice. Rosining too much can create excess buildup.

2. Shoulder Rest

- **Comfort and Stability:** A shoulder rest gives support and comfort while playing. It also ensures your fiddle stays securely in place, so you can focus on your performance.

- **Different Styles:** Shoulder rests come in various styles and sizes. Explore different options to find one that suits your shoulder and playing style.

3. Tuner and Metronome

- **Precision Tools:** A tuner and metronome are invaluable for maintaining pitch accuracy and rhythm. Many tuners also have metronome functions, making them a versatile addition to your kit.

4. Fiddle Case

- **Protection on the Go:** A high-quality fiddle case is a must for safeguarding your instrument during transportation. Hard-shell cases offer superior protection against bumps and temperature fluctuations.

- **Hygrometer:** Some cases come equipped with a built-in hygrometer to monitor humidity levels, ensuring your fiddle remains in optimal condition.

5. Extra Strings

- **Always Be Prepared:** Strings can break unexpectedly. Having a spare set of strings on hand, along with the tools to change them, ensures you're always ready to play.

6. Cleaning Supplies

- **Maintaining Your Fiddle:** Soft, lint-free cloths and cleaning solutions designed for fiddles help keep your instrument looking and sounding its best.

7. Mute

- **Tone Control:** A mute is handy when you need to practice quietly or dampen the fiddle's tone for specific musical effects.

Tailoring Your Accessories to Your Style

Every fiddler is an individual, and your accessories should reflect your personality and playing style.

- **Genre-Specific Accessories:** Depending on the genre you play, you may find that certain accessories are more suited to your needs. For example, a bluegrass fiddler might opt for a different bow and rosin than a classical violinist.

- **Experimentation:** Don't hesitate to experiment with different combinations of bows, rosins, and accessories. It's through this exploration that you'll discover the perfect blend that unlocks your fiddle's true voice.

Selecting the right bow and accessories for your fiddle is deeply personal and rewarding. These elements are extensions of your musical expression. Take your time to explore different options, test various bows, and tailor your accessory selection to match your playing style. By doing so, you'll heighten your playing experience and craft a unique and resonant voice for your fiddle that will captivate audiences and enrich your musical journey.

Chapter 3: Holding and Tuning Your Fiddle

How you cradle your fiddle and position it against your body will impact your playing technique and comfort. Tuning, the cornerstone of melodic harmony, is a key focus. This chapter will demystify fiddle tuning, guiding you through electronic tuners and helping you achieve that perfect pitch. After all, a well-tuned fiddle is the gateway to the crisp, resonant tones that define this beloved instrument.

Techniques for Holding and Positioning

When playing the fiddle, your technique is not solely about using the bow or fingering the strings. It begins with something more foundational: how you hold and position the fiddle itself. It might seem simple, but it affects your playing ability, comfort, and even your sound quality.

Holding the Fiddle: A Delicate Balance

6. A fiddle must be held firmly but softly. Source: https://unsplash.com/photos/person-playing-brown-violin-SgthjoHW6ec

A fiddle must be held firmly but softly. Here are the key components of the fiddle hold:

1. **The Chinrest:** Start by resting your chin on the chinrest at the bottom of the fiddle. Your chin should be positioned near the tailpiece, the bottom end of the fiddle. This point of contact helps to anchor the fiddle against your body.

2. **The Shoulder Rest:** The shoulder rest, usually attached to the back of the fiddle, provides crucial support. It keeps the fiddle from sliding around while allowing for a comfortable inclination angle. The height and position of the shoulder rest can be adjusted to suit your comfort and playing style.

3. **The Left Hand:** Your left hand will come into play once you've secured the fiddle with your chin and shoulder. The thumb should rest against the back of the

fiddle's neck while the fingers arch over the fingerboard, ready to press down on the strings. This hand positioning is vital for proper finger placement and intonation.

4. **The Right Hand:** The right hand is responsible for bowing, but it also plays a role in holding the fiddle. Your right thumb should lightly touch the bottom of the fingerboard, and your fingers should naturally curve around the bow, which lets you bow fluidly while maintaining a stable grip on the fiddle.

Optimal Position

Once you've established the basic hold, it's time to position the fiddle properly against your body. This influences both comfort and sound quality. Here's how to do it:

1. **Stand or Sit up Straight:** Good posture is the foundation of proper fiddle positioning. Whether standing or sitting, keep your back straight, and your shoulders relaxed. This ensures that the fiddle aligns with your body's natural contours.

2. **Balance and Tilt:** The fiddle should be balanced between your chin and shoulder. The tilt angle depends on your preference and comfort. Some fiddlers prefer a slightly more vertical angle, while others tilt it slightly forward. Experiment to find what works best.

3. **Height Adjustment:** The height of the fiddle can also be adjusted to suit your body. You can raise or lower the shoulder rest so that the fiddle is at a comfortable height. Ideally, the fiddle's fingerboard should align with your left hand, allowing for easy finger placement.

Common Mistakes

- **Clamping the Fiddle:** Avoid gripping the fiddle too tightly with your chin and shoulder. This causes tension in your neck and shoulders, which could cause discomfort and potentially affect your playing. Find a balance where the fiddle is secure but not clamped in a death grip.

- **Leaning over the Fiddle:** Resist the temptation to hunch over the fiddle. Maintaining good posture is essential for long-term comfort and endurance. Keep your back straight and your head upright to avoid straining your neck and back.

- **Neglecting the Shoulder Rest:** Don't underestimate the importance of the shoulder rest. It provides critical support for the fiddle and can significantly boost your playing experience. Adjust it to fit your body comfortably.

Practice Makes Perfect

Like any skill, mastering the art of holding and positioning the fiddle takes practice. Spend time adjusting and readjusting until you find the sweet spot that feels comfortable and allows for fluid playing. Experiment with different shoulder rest heights, tilt angles, and chinrest positions to discover what works best.

As you practice, pay attention to any tension or discomfort in your body. This is a valuable indicator of an improper hold or position. Don't be afraid to make small adjustments as needed to alleviate any discomfort.

How you hold and position your instrument is the foundation upon which your musical journey is built. A solid fiddle hold and proper positioning enhance your comfort and impact the quality of sound you produce. So, take the time to learn and refine these techniques, and remember that practice is your ally in achieving the perfect fiddle hold. With dedication and patience, you'll be well on your way to becoming a master.

Understanding Fiddle Tuning and Electronic Tuners

The fiddle, with its soul-stirring melodies and foot-tapping rhythms, has enchanted musicians and audiences for centuries. But to produce those captivating tunes, one must embark on a quest for perfect fiddle tuning. This journey involves understanding the intricacies of tuning and utilizing an invaluable tool: the electronic tuner.

The Basics of Fiddle Tuning

Before you dive into the world of electronic tuners, start with the fundamental principles of fiddle tuning. The fiddle, like many stringed instruments, is typically tuned to a standard set of pitches. The most common tuning for a fiddle is G-D-A-E, starting from the lowest-pitched string (G) to the highest (E).

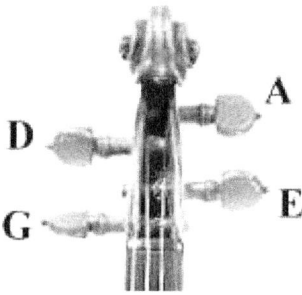

7.   *The fiddle is typically tuned to a standard set of pitches. Source: https://commons.wikimedia.org/wiki/File:Violin_peg_strings.jpg*

- **G String:** The lowest string is often called the "bottom string." It produces a deep, resonant sound and is the foundation for many fiddle tunes.

- **D String:** The second string from the bottom. It adds a rich harmony to your fiddling and complements the G string beautifully.

- **A String:** The third string from the bottom. It has a brighter tone and is often used for melodies that require a crisp, clear sound.

- **E String:** The highest string. It provides a brilliant, airy quality and is frequently used for playing high-pitched melodies.

The Importance of Proper Tuning

Why is proper tuning so crucial for fiddle players? Simply put, it's the key to producing beautiful, harmonious music. A well-tuned fiddle ensures that your notes are in pitch, allowing you to play in tune with other musicians and create melodies that resonate with your audience. Without accurate tuning, your fiddle could sound dissonant and off-putting.

Manual Tuning vs. Electronic Tuning

Traditionally, fiddlers rely on their ears and experience to tune their instruments manually. While this method is effective for experienced players, it can be challenging for beginners or those with less developed musical ears. This is where electronic tuners come into play. Electronic tuners are small, portable devices that use technology to help you achieve precise tuning. They work by detecting the pitch of your fiddle strings and providing visual or auditory feedback to guide you in adjusting the tension of each string.

Using an Electronic Tuner

It's time to unravel the mystery of using an electronic tuner to tune your fiddle:

1. **Choose the Right Tuner:** There is a wide range of electronic tuners available, from clip-on tuners that attach to your fiddle to pedal tuners for stage use. Select a tuner that suits your preferences and needs.

2. **Clip It on:** If using a clip-on tuner, attach it to your fiddle's headstock, ensuring it's securely in place.

3. **Select the Correct Mode:** Most tuners offer different modes for various instruments. Make sure you choose the violin or fiddle mode to get accurate results.

4. **Pluck the String:** Pluck one string at a time, starting with the G string. The tuner will display the string's pitch, indicating whether it's too high, too low, or in tune.

5. **Adjust the Tension:** Use the tuning pegs on your fiddle's scroll to adjust the string's tension. Turn the peg clockwise to raise the pitch and counterclockwise to lower it. Be patient and make small adjustments to avoid over-tightening.

6. **Repeat for Each String:** Tune each string one by one, moving from G to D, then A, and finally, E. Use the tuner until all strings are perfectly in tune.

7. **Fine-Tuning:** Once you've tuned all the strings, play open strings and listen carefully. Sometimes, the tuner will indicate that a string is in tune, but your ear still detects slight discrepancies. Fine-tune by ear to ensure optimal harmony.

Tips for Using Electronic Tuners

To make the most of your electronic tuner, consider these tips:

- **Practice Regularly:** Make tuning a part of your practice routine. Frequent tuning maintains the tonal quality of the instrument and trains your ear.

- **Check Intonation:** In addition to tuning, periodically check the intonation of your fiddle. This ensures that the notes remain in tune up and down the fingerboard.

- **Use a Reference Pitch:** If you have access to a reference pitch, such as a tuning fork or a piano, you can use it to set the initial pitch for your G string. Then, tune the other strings relative to the G string.

- **Learn to Tune by Ear:** While electronic tuners are incredibly helpful, developing your ear for tuning is a valuable skill for any musician. Try tuning without a tuner occasionally to focus your ear.

8. Try tuning without a tuner occasionally to focus your ear. Source: https://pixabay.com/vectors/sound-listening-man-ear-hearing-159915/

Tuning your fiddle is not just a necessary chore, it's a vital step in creating beautiful music. Understanding the basics of fiddle tuning and harnessing the power of an electronic tuner can elevate your playing to new heights. Whether you're a seasoned fiddler or just starting your musical journey, the combination of knowledge and technology will help you unlock the full potential of this timeless instrument.

Keeping Your Fiddle in Tune for Optimal Sound Quality

The sweet, melodic strains of a well-tuned fiddle transport listeners to another world. Yet, maintaining that pristine sound quality requires more than just a one-time tuning. To keep your fiddle singing beautifully, you must understand the factors that affect its tuning stability and put them into practice for its care.

1. **The Nature of Fiddle Tuning:** Before you dive into the strategies for maintaining fiddle tuning, it's crucial to understand why a fiddle may go out of tune in the first place. Several factors contribute to this phenomenon:

   - **Tension and Temperature:** Your fiddle's strings are under constant tension, which can be affected by temperature changes. Cold weather causes the strings to contract, while heat makes them expand. These fluctuations lead to tuning instability.

   - **Playing and Handling:** Playing the fiddle, including pressing the strings with your fingers and bowing, exerts pressure on the strings, causing them to stretch and detune slightly.

- **String Aging:** Over time, fiddle strings degrade, losing their elasticity and tonal quality. Old strings are more likely to go out of tune.

- **Pegs and Fine Tuners:** The pegs used for tuning the fiddle can slip if they are not properly seated or too tight. Fine tuners, while helpful, affect tuning if they are not adjusted correctly.

2. **Establish a Tuning Routine:** Consistency is key in maintaining your fiddle's tuning. Create a routine where you check and adjust your fiddle's tuning before each practice session or performance. It ensures that your fiddle sounds its best and helps you become more attuned to its nuances.

3. **Use Quality Strings:** Invest in high-quality strings for your fiddle. Well-made strings not only produce better tone but also hold their tuning more effectively. Keep an eye on your strings' condition and replace them as they wear out or lose their tonal quality.

4. **Fine-Tuning with Fine Tuners:** Many fiddlers use fine tuners, small mechanical devices attached to the tailpiece, to make precise tuning adjustments. These fine tuners are especially useful for making small changes to the pitch without turning the pegs. Ensure that your fine-tuners are in good condition and that they move smoothly.

5. **Peg Maintenance:** Proper maintenance of your pegs is essential for tuning stability. Apply peg compound or peg paste to the pegs' contact points to reduce friction. If a peg is slipping, have it professionally adjusted or replaced. Remember, pegs should turn smoothly but not loosely.

6. **Climate Considerations:** Extreme temperature changes wreak havoc on your fiddle's tuning. Store your fiddle in a stable environment with constant temperature and humidity levels. Consider using a humidifier or dehumidifier to maintain ideal conditions, especially in dry or humid climates.

7. **Stretch Your Strings:** New strings, or strings that haven't been played in a while, are prone to slipping out of tune. To mitigate this, gently stretch each string by pulling it away from the fingerboard several times after tuning, and tune the string again. This helps the strings settle and hold their pitch more effectively.

8. **Monitor Your Tailpiece:** Check the tailpiece of your fiddle for any signs of wear or damage. A cracked or worn tailpiece can affect your fiddle's tuning stability. If you notice any issues, consider having it repaired or replaced.

9. **Regular Maintenance:** Periodically, take your fiddle to a luthier or experienced instrument technician for professional setup and maintenance. They can ensure that all components of your fiddle, including the soundpost and bridge, are in prime condition, contributing to better tuning stability and sound quality.

10. **Tuning Apps and Electronic Tuners:** Consider using tuning apps or electronic tuners to aid in the tuning process. These tools provide accurate visual or auditory feedback, making it easier to achieve precise tuning. However, remember that your ear should always be your guide, especially for fine-tuning and achieving the best sound quality.

A well-tuned fiddle is a gateway to musical enchantment. By understanding the factors that affect fiddle tuning and applying sound maintenance practices, you can ensure that your instrument consistently delivers the best sound quality possible. Treat your fiddle carefully, practice good tuning habits, and seek professional assistance when needed. With dedication and attention to detail, your fiddle will remain in tune and continue to weave its magical melodies for years to come.

Chapter 4: Basic Bowing Techniques

The bow is your trusty companion for your fiddle, the conduit through which you weave your musical magic. To master this instrument, you must understand its intricacies. The bow comprises the stick, the frog, and the hair, each playing an integral role in your music.

This chapter explores the art of basic bowing techniques, teaching you the secrets to crafting a clear and even sound that will make your fiddle sing. You'll dive deep into the world of the fiddle's bow, exploring its various components, their roles, and how they work together harmoniously to produce beautiful melodies.

The Bow: A Symphony in Simplicity

At first glance, a fiddle bow may appear deceptively simple, consisting of just a stick, a frog, and a bundle of horsehair. However, mastery of these elements and their intricate interactions separates a novice from a seasoned fiddler.

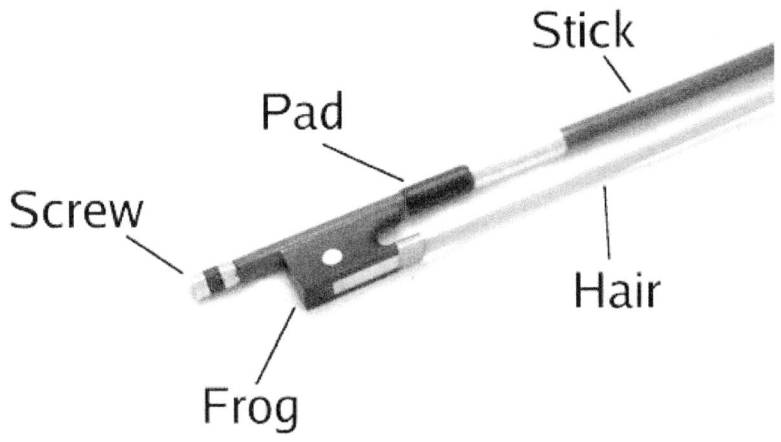

9. A fiddle bow may appear deceptively simple. Source: Kbh3rd, CC BY-SA 3.0 <http://creativecommons.org/licenses/by-sa/3.0/>, via Wikimedia Commons: https://commons.wikimedia.org/wiki/File:Violin_bow_parts.jpg

The Stick

The stick is the backbone of the bow. Typically crafted from high-quality wood, it serves as the main structural component and the conduit through which the fiddler imparts control and expression to their music. The stick is curved to create tension when drawn across the strings, resulting in the production of sound.

Different types of wood are used in bow making, each with unique characteristics that influence the bow's tone and performance. For example, pernambuco wood is highly regarded for its resonance and flexibility, making it a popular choice among professional fiddlers. Brazilwood, a more affordable alternative, offers good quality for intermediate players. The choice of wood significantly influences the overall sound and playability of the bow.

The Frog

Moving down the bow from the stick, you encounter the frog, a crucial component responsible for adjusting the bow's tension and holding the horsehair in place. The frog is made of wood or sometimes synthetic material, and it features a mechanism that tightens or loosens the hair, affecting the bow's response.

To adjust the tension, players turn the screw located on the underside of the frog. This helps them to find the sweet spot that suits their playing style and the specific demands of the music they're performing. Proper tension ensures the bow responds effectively to the player's control, producing clear and expressive tones.

The Horsehair

The final component of the bow is the horsehair, which extends from the frog to the tip of the stick. The horsehair's interaction with the strings is where the magic happens. When drawn across the strings, the horsehair grips them, causing them to vibrate and produce sound.

Quality matters when it comes to horsehair. High-quality horsehair is strong, resilient, and responsive, giving you a more nuanced and expressive playing experience. Professional-grade bows often feature the finest horsehair, ensuring the fiddler achieves a full range of dynamics and tonal colors.

The Harmony of Components

Now that you've examined the individual components of the bow, it's time to explore how they work together in harmony to produce the enchanting sounds that are synonymous with the fiddle.

When a fiddler draws the bow across the strings, the horsehair grips them, setting them in motion. This motion creates vibrations in the strings, which are then amplified by the fiddle's body, producing sound. The stick's curvature and flexibility play a vital role in regulating the pressure exerted on the strings, allowing the fiddler to control the volume, tone, and articulation of the notes.

The frog, with its ability to adjust tension, enables the fiddler to fine-tune the bow's response. A looser bow produces a gentler, mellower sound, ideal for slow, lyrical passages, while a tighter bow creates a brighter, more assertive tone, perfect for lively jigs and reels. It's through this delicate balance of tension that the fiddler achieves the desired expressiveness in their playing.

Choosing the Right Bow

Selecting the right bow for your fiddling journey is a crucial decision. The bow's characteristics, such as its weight, balance, and flexibility, work together to shape your playing experience.

- **Try before You Buy:** Whenever possible, try out different bows to see which one feels most comfortable and responsive in your hands. The perfect bow is a deeply personal choice.

- **Consider Your Style:** Different styles of fiddling may require different bow characteristics. For example, classical fiddlers prefer a bow with a more pronounced curve for nuanced dynamics, while bluegrass fiddlers opt for a stiffer, flatter bow for fast-paced tunes.

- **Seek Expert Advice:** Consult with experienced fiddlers or bow makers for guidance. You'll get expert advice as well as recommendations based on your skill level and musical goals.

- **Budget Wisely:** Bows come in a wide price range. While a high-quality bow can make a noticeable difference in your playing, there are also excellent options available for those on a budget. Explore your options and invest wisely.

The bow is your key to unlocking the beauty and expressiveness of the instrument. Understanding its parts, from the stick to the frog and the horsehair, empowers you to craft melodies that resonate with emotion and precision.

As you embark on your journey to master the fiddle's bow, remember that it's not just the individual components but their harmonious interplay that creates the magic. Experiment with different bows, explore their individual characteristics and let your bow become an extension of your musical voice.

Techniques for Producing a Clear and Even Sound on the Fiddle

Playing the fiddle is an art form that hinges on producing a melodic, crystal clear, and perfectly even sound. Achieving this level of precision requires a deep understanding of bowing techniques, the correct posture, and unwavering practice.

The Foundation: Proper Bow Hold

Before you dive into the nuances of bowing techniques, start with the foundation of your bow hold. How you grip the bow dramatically influences your ability to produce a clear and even sound.

10. How you grip the bow dramatically influences your ability to produce a clear and even sound. Source: https://www.pexels.com/photo/violinist-playing-in-the-field-18464432/

1. **Firm but Gentle:** Hold the bow firmly enough to maintain control but not so tightly that it restricts the bow's movement.

2. **Thumb Placement:** Your thumb should rest on the back of the bow, slightly bent. Avoid pressing it too hard. A relaxed thumb allows for flexibility in bowing.

3. **Fingers Positioning:** The fingers of your bow hand should be gently curved and rest lightly on the bow's

frog. This allows for flexibility and finesse in your bowing movements.

Bowing Techniques for Clarity and Evenness

1. **Straight Bowing:** Maintaining a straight bow is fundamental to achieving clarity and evenness in your sound. Imagine an imaginary line running parallel to the bridge of your fiddle. Your bow should move parallel to this line as you play.

    - **Practice Tip:** Place a thin strip of masking tape on your fiddle's strings near the bridge as a visual guide for keeping your bow straight. Aim to bow within this boundary to develop muscle memory.

2. **Bow Speed and Pressure Control:** Controlling bow speed and pressure is where the magic happens. Different passages and musical styles require varying combinations of speed and pressure for clear and even sound.

    - **Slow and Gentle:** For slow, lyrical passages, use slow bow strokes with gentle pressure. Focus on drawing out each note to create a rich and expressive sound.

    - **Fast and Light:** In lively tunes or when playing staccato, use faster bow strokes with lighter pressure. This produces a crisp, articulate sound.

    - **Smooth Transitions:** When shifting between bow strokes, keep your speed and pressure consistent to avoid abrupt changes in volume or tone.

3. **Bow Placement:** How you place your bow on the strings plays a crucial role in playing clearly and evenly.

- **Playing Near the Bridge:** Playing closer to the bridge emphasizes a brighter, more focused tone, ideal for cutting through in ensemble playing or adding brilliance to a melody.

- **Playing Closer to the Fingerboard:** Moving your bow closer to the fingerboard produces a mellower, softer tone, suitable for creating a warm and gentle sound, often used in slow ballads.

- **Experimentation:** To master bow placement, experiment with different positions along the string. Find the sweet spot that best suits the mood and style of the music you're playing.

4. **Bow Tilt:** Bow tilt refers to the angle at which the bow hair contacts the strings. Controlling bow tilt can help you produce a consistent, even sound.

- **Flat Bow:** For an even sound, maintain a flat bow with the hair evenly contacting the strings. It's a good default position for many playing situations.

- **Tilted Bow:** Tilting the bow slightly towards the fingerboard can soften the sound, which is ideal for achieving a sweeter tone in certain passages.

- **Tilted Bow Away from Fingerboard:** Tilting the bow away from the fingerboard can produce a more aggressive, biting tone, useful for adding emphasis or drama to your playing.

5. **Developing Your Ear:** Producing a clear and even sound on the fiddle is not just about technique. It's also about developing your ear. Listening intently to your

playing and seeking feedback from experienced musicians can help you refine your sound.

- **Record Yourself:** You can have an objective assessment of the sound you produce when you record your session.

- **Play Along with Others:** Playing with fellow musicians will give you valuable feedback and help you develop a sense of ensemble playing, where clarity and evenness are crucial.

- **Seek Guidance:** Don't hesitate to take lessons or attend workshops with experienced fiddlers who can provide personalized guidance and tips.

Mastering the art of producing a clear and even sound when bowing on the fiddle is a journey that requires dedication, patience, and a keen ear. It's about refining your technique, honing your bow control, and infusing your playing with emotion and expression. Consistent, focused practice sessions will yield noticeable improvements over time.

Mastering the Art of Bow Control and Dynamics

When you pick up a fiddle, you hold within your grasp not just an instrument but a vessel for self-expression. The secret to unlocking the full potential of the fiddle lies in your ability to control the bow with finesse and master the art of dynamics.

The Foundation: Bow Grip and Hand Position

Before you dive into the nuances of bow control and dynamics, it's essential to establish a solid foundation by focusing on your bow grip and hand position.

- **Balanced Bow Hold:** Ensure your bow grip is balanced, with fingers lightly but firmly pressing against the bow. Your thumb should rest on the back of the bow, providing support without squeezing too tightly.

- **Hand Position:** Maintain a relaxed hand position with gently curved fingers. Avoid unnecessary tension, as it can block your ability to control the bow's movements.

Bow Control: The Key to Precision

1. **Bow Distribution:** Bow control begins with understanding how to distribute the bow across the strings. Different sections of the bow produce various dynamics:

   - **Frog (Near the Hand):** Using the bow closest to the frog produces a rich, powerful sound. This section is excellent for accents and when you need to make a strong musical statement.

   - **Middle:** The middle section offers balanced control, suitable for most playing situations. It allows you to produce even dynamics with ease.

   - **Tip (Far from the Hand):** The bow's tip is perfect for creating delicate, soft sounds, ideal for pianissimo passages and adding subtle nuances to your playing.

2. **Bow Speed Variation:** Varying the speed of your bow strokes is essential for achieving dynamics.

   - **Slower Bow Strokes:** To produce a softer, quieter sound, slow down your bow speed while keeping an even pressure. This technique works well for legato passages and expressing vulnerability in your music.

- **Faster Bow Strokes:** For louder, more intense dynamics, increase your bow speed. It's effective for creating dramatic, emotional crescendos and adding excitement to your performance.

3. **Bow Pressure:** Bow pressure is the weight you apply to the strings with your bow. To achieve different dynamics, you must learn to adjust bow pressure seamlessly:

- **Light Pressure:** When using light bow pressure, the strings vibrate less vigorously, producing a quieter sound. This technique is perfect for pianissimo and mezzo-piano passages.

- **Medium Pressure:** A medium bow pressure gives you a balanced sound, suitable for most musical phrases. It allows you to maintain control while producing a clear and even tone.

- **Heavy Pressure:** For fortissimo and dramatic sections, apply heavy pressure to the strings. This will make them vibrate vigorously, creating a powerful, intense sound.

Dynamics: Conveying Emotion through Music

Dynamic range is the canvas on which you paint emotions with your fiddle. Here's how to harness dynamics to convey feelings in your music:

1. **Start with the Basics:** Begin your journey into dynamics by practicing simple exercises that involve gradually increasing and decreasing volume. Start with

scales, playing each note softly and then louder before reversing the process.

11. Start with scales, playing each note softly and then louder before reversing the process. Source: https://unsplash.com/photos/grayscale-photo-of-person-playing-violin-WYiIkQFclA4

2. **Listen Actively:** Become an active listener. Pay close attention to the nuances in your favorite fiddle pieces, noting how the fiddler uses bow control and dynamics to convey emotion. Try to replicate these techniques in your playing.

3. **Embrace Phrasing:** Dynamics are closely tied to phrasing. Think of your musical phrases as sentences with punctuation. Begin softly, build to a climax, and then release tension by softening your sound. This adds drama and expression to your playing.

4. **Practice Crescendos and Diminuendos:** Crescendos (gradual increases in volume) and diminuendos (gradual decreases in volume) are

fundamental dynamic techniques. Practice them on scales and simple melodies to develop control and sensitivity.

The Road to Mastery

Developing bow control and mastering dynamics on the fiddle is a journey that requires time, patience, and dedication. Here are some tips to help you along the way:

- **Record Yourself:** You can see where you need to improve by assessing your playing when you record the session. This is a great way to figure out how to get the best out of your dynamics and how to hold your bow.

- **Experiment:** Don't be afraid to experiment with different bowing techniques and dynamics. Try playing the same passage, changing the dynamics to find out what resonates most with you emotionally.

- **Seek Guidance:** You should definitely look for a teacher who can guide you when it comes to how to position the bow and the overall dynamics.

- **Practice Regularly:** Consistent practice is the key to mastering bow control and dynamics. Dedicate time each day to honing your skills, and you'll see significant progress over time.

As you continue your fiddling journey, remember that bow control and dynamics are the vehicles through which you express the heart and soul of your music. With each stroke of the bow, you can convey a range of emotions, from joy to sorrow, excitement to tranquility.

By mastering the art of bow control and dynamics, you enhance your technical proficiency and deepen your connection with your instrument and audience. So, pick up your fiddle, embrace the nuances of bowing, and let your music tell a story that resonates with clarity and emotion. With practice and dedication, you'll become a fiddler capable of moving hearts and stirring souls with your musical prowess.

Chapter 5: Learning Essential Fiddle Fingerings

In fiddling, mastery begins with the fingers. Learning essential fiddle fingering is the foundation upon which every aspiring player builds their craft. In this chapter, you'll explore the intricate art of finger positions and fingering techniques, unveiling the secrets behind producing the sweetest melodies and vibrant harmonies. You'll discover the essential fingerings for scales, dissect their nuances, and demonstrate how to memorize and practice them effectively. Along the way, you'll unravel the magic of developing finger agility, enabling you to glide seamlessly between notes.

Introduction to Finger Positions and Fingering

Whether you're a budding fiddler or a seasoned player looking to refine your skills, understanding the intricacies of finger positions and techniques is the first step toward becoming a true virtuoso. It's the very essence of creating enchanting music that stirs the soul.

The Importance of Finger Positions

Before you delve into the intricacies of fingering techniques, you must learn the basic finger positions. In fiddling, like with other stringed instruments, the placement of your fingers on the strings plays a pivotal role in the sound you produce. Each finger has its designated role, and understanding these positions is fundamental.

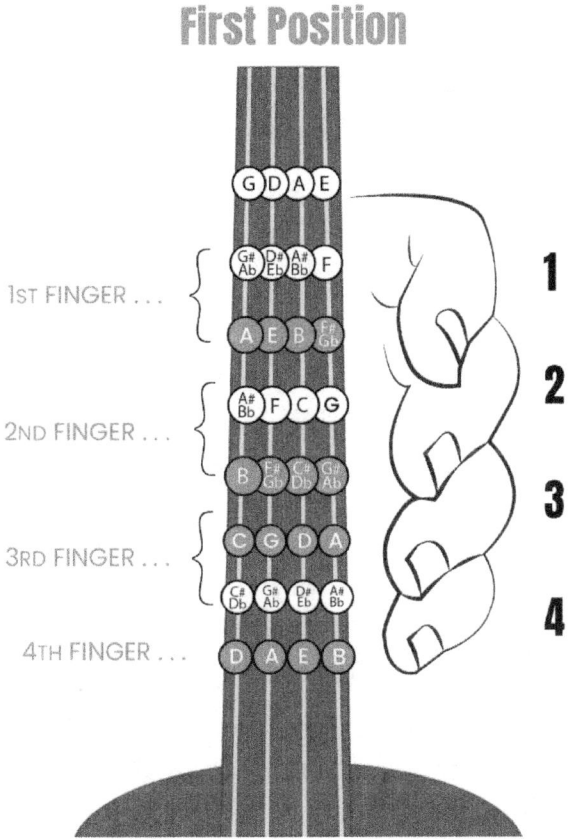

12. *The placement of your fingers on the strings plays a pivotal role in the sound you produce. Source: https://violinspiration.com/wp-content/uploads/finger-placement-on-violin-first-position-fingering.jpg*

1. **First Finger (Index Finger):** This finger covers the first and sometimes the second or third notes on a string. It's your go-to for creating clear, crisp notes.

2. **Second Finger (Middle Finger):** The second finger hits the second and sometimes third notes on a string. It's all about precision and accuracy.

3. **Third Finger (Ring Finger):** When you need to reach those higher notes on a string, the third finger comes into play. It adds versatility to your playing.

4. **Fourth Finger (Pinky):** Although the fourth finger isn't used as frequently, it's indispensable for reaching the highest notes on a string. It adds depth to your repertoire.

Understanding these finger positions sets the stage for mastering the art of fiddling.

Fingering Techniques

- **Vibrato:** Vibrato is the key to infusing your fiddling with emotion and depth. It involves a slight, controlled oscillation of the pitch of a note. To achieve vibrato, gently rock your finger back and forth while maintaining contact with the string. The result is a rich, expressive sound that conveys a wide range of feelings, from joy to melancholy.

- **Slurs:** Slurs are a graceful technique used to transition between notes smoothly. They involve playing two or more consecutive notes with a single bow stroke, often while changing finger positions. To execute a slur, maintain steady bow pressure and adjust your finger placement fluidly. Slurs add a sense of elegance and fluidity to your playing.

- **Double Stops:** This is when you play 2 strings simultaneously. Clean double stops require precise finger positioning and bow control. For example, you can play a melody on one string while harmonizing with another, adding depth and complexity to your music.

- **Finger Rolls:** Finger rolls are an embellishment that adds character to your melodies. They involve swiftly rolling your finger across the string to create a rapid succession of notes. This technique can add flair to your tunes, particularly in upbeat or lively pieces.

- **Position Shifts:** To explore the full range of the fiddle's capabilities, you must navigate position shifts. This involves smoothly transitioning your hand and finger positions up or down the neck of the fiddle to play different notes. Position shifts need precision and practice but open up a world of musical possibilities.

Putting It All Together

Mastering finger positions and fingering techniques is an exercise that requires dedication and patience. Start by practicing your finger positions, ensuring each note is clear and resonant. As you become comfortable with the basics, gradually incorporate fingering techniques into your practice routine. Experiment with vibrato to infuse your music with emotion, use slurs to create smooth transitions, and explore the world of double stops, finger rolls, and position shifts to expand your repertoire.

Remember, the key to mastery is practice. Spend time each day refining your finger positions and experimenting with different fingering techniques. Over time, you'll discover your unique voice as a fiddler and create music that captivates both your audience and your own heart.

Memorizing and Practicing Essential Scale Fingerings

Mastering scales is like learning the alphabet of a language. Musical scales are the building blocks for creating captivating melodies and harmonies. To bring these scales to life, you must memorize and practice essential fingerings. This requires patience, dedication, and a deep appreciation for the art of the fiddle.

The Foundation of Melodic Expression

Before diving into the specifics of memorizing and practicing fingering, first, you must understand why scales are so vital for fiddlers. Scales are the fundamental framework for music, offering a sequence of notes that form the basis of melodies and harmonies. They are the foundation upon which musical expression is built.

The Role of Muscle Memory

Memorizing scales on the fiddle is like teaching your fingers a dance. It's all about muscle memory, which is the ability your brain has to remember specific movements without conscious thought. When you practice scales consistently, your fingers become attuned to the patterns, making it easier to navigate the fretboard effortlessly.

The Art of Memorization

1. **Visualizing the Scale:** Begin by visualizing the scale you want to memorize. Whether it's the major scale, minor scale, or a more exotic mode, picture the sequence of notes in your mind. This mental

preparation will help you anticipate the fingerings as you play.

2. **Start Slowly:** When you first tackle a new scale, start slowly. Break it down into manageable segments and play each section repeatedly until you can navigate it smoothly. As you become more comfortable, gradually increase the tempo.

3. **Use Mnemonics:** Mnemonics are a powerful tool for memorization. Create acronyms or phrases to remember the order of notes in the scale. For example, the mnemonic "Every Good Boy Does Fine" can help you recall the lines from the bottom to the top of the treble clef in sheet music.

4. **Practice in All Keys:** Don't limit yourself to one key. Practice scales in different keys to expand your musical vocabulary. Each key presents a unique challenge and helps you develop a more versatile fingerboard knowledge.

The Art of Practice

- **Consistency Is Key:** Regular practice is the key to mastering scales. Make sure that you commit part of your session to practicing the scales. Consistency builds muscle memory over time.

- **Use a Metronome:** A metronome is your best friend when practicing scales. It helps you maintain a steady tempo and ensures that you're playing with precision. Gradually increase the metronome speed as you improve.

13. A metronome is your best friend when practicing scales. Source: Paco from Badajoz, España, CC BY 2.0 <https://creativecommons.org/licenses/by/2.0>, via Wikimedia Commons: https://commons.wikimedia.org/wiki/File:Wittner_metronome.jpg

- **Focus on Finger Placement:** How your fingers are positioned is crucial. Ensure that each note is clear and resonant. Precision in fingering is essential for scales to sound their best.

- **Experiment with Bowing Techniques:** Scales aren't just about your left hand. Your bowing hand plays a crucial role, too. Experiment with different bowing techniques, such as slurs and staccato, to add dynamics and character to your scale practice.

The Reward of Mastery

As you commit to memorizing and practicing essential fingerings for different scales, you'll unlock many musical possibilities on the fiddle. Scales will no longer be mere exercises but tools for creative expression. You'll find that your ability to improvise, compose, and interpret music grows immensely.

Beyond the technical benefits, mastering scales offers a profound sense of accomplishment. It's akin to mastering the grammar and vocabulary of a new language, enabling you to communicate your musical thoughts fluently and eloquently.

Developing Finger Agility for Smooth Transitions

The ability to create seamless transitions between notes is nothing short of magical. It transforms a melody from a series of disconnected sounds into a flowing, dynamic narrative. Achieving this fluidity requires a fundamental skill: finger agility.

The Essence of Finger Agility

At its core, finger agility is about the skill and flexibility of your fingers on the fingerboard. It's the capacity to move effortlessly and swiftly from one note to another, allowing you to connect notes, create melodic lines, and express the full range of emotions through your playing.

Finger Exercises

- **Finger Independence:** Begin your journey to finger agility with exercises that focus on finger independence. Each finger should be able to move on its own, without being constrained by the others. Try this: place your first finger on a string, hold it down, and lift and lower your other fingers independently. This exercise encourages agility and control.

- **Finger Stretching:** Stretching your fingers is vital for flexibility. Place your fingers on the fingerboard, starting with the first and second fingers on adjacent strings. Slowly spread them apart and then bring them back together. Repeat this exercise regularly to improve finger reach.

- **Finger Rolling:** Finger agility also involves rolling your fingers swiftly across the strings. Practice rolling your fingers from the first finger to the fourth and back again. This movement helps develop the skills required for quick transitions.

Scales and Arpeggios

Scales and arpeggios are invaluable tools for enhancing finger agility. They not only teach you the structure of different keys but also encourage smooth finger transitions. Start with simple scales and arpeggios and gradually work up to more complex ones.

- **Scale Runs:** Practice running up and down scales smoothly. Ensure that the positioning of your fingers is correct so that the notes are played clearly. As you become more proficient, increase your speed while maintaining precision.

- **Arpeggio Patterns:** Arpeggios consist of the first, third, and fifth notes of a scale and are essential for transitioning between chords and creating harmonic progressions. Practice different arpeggio patterns, focusing on the agility required to move from one chord to another seamlessly.

Shifting and Position Changes

One of the hallmarks of a skilled fiddler is the ability to navigate the fingerboard effortlessly. This involves shifting and changing hand positions while maintaining a smooth and uninterrupted music flow.

- **Sliding Technique:** Practice sliding your fingers along the strings to change positions. Start with simple slides, moving from one position to another and back. As you become more comfortable, incorporate this technique into your playing to transition between different parts of a piece.

- **Guided Position Changes:** Include guided position changes into your practice routine. This involves visualizing the next position, moving your hand while maintaining contact with the fingerboard, and then landing smoothly on the desired notes. Guided position changes are crucial for avoiding abrupt shifts that can disrupt the flow of your music.

Bowing Techniques

While finger agility primarily involves the left hand, don't forget the importance of bowing techniques in achieving smooth transitions. Proper bow control and coordination with finger movements are essential for creating seamless phrasing and articulation.

- **Bow Direction:** Experiment with different bowing directions (up-bow and down-bow) to complement your finger transitions. The bow should align with the direction of your finger movement, ensuring that each note flows naturally into the next.

- **Staccato and Legato:** Practice staccato (short, detached bow strokes) and legato (smooth, connected bow strokes) to vary the articulation of your notes. These techniques add depth and character to your transitions, allowing you to convey various emotions.

The Joy of Fluid Transitions

Developing finger agility is a gradual process that requires patience and persistence. Start by practicing slowly and with precision. When you become confident enough, you can increase the speed. The goal is to achieve fluid transitions while maintaining accuracy.

As you commit to developing finger agility for smooth transitions on the fiddle, you'll discover a profound sense of joy in your music. The ability to connect notes seamlessly opens doors to creative expression and allows you to communicate your emotions through your playing.

Remember, the journey to finger agility is a personal one, and progress will vary from person to person. Embrace the process, celebrate your milestones, and revel in the beauty of your fiddle's melodies as they flow effortlessly from your fingertips. With dedication and practice, you'll unlock the secret to those mesmerizing, smooth transitions that captivate the hearts of both performers and listeners.

Chapter 6: Playing Your First Fiddle Tunes

Playing your first fiddle tunes is a thrilling journey into the heart of traditional music. It's like stepping into a time machine that transports you to rustic barn dances and cozy campfires under a starry sky. To embark on this musical adventure, you'll need a trusty fiddle and a little patience.

Fiddling is as much about storytelling as it is about music. Each tune carries a piece of history and culture, and as you play, you become a part of that timeless tradition. So, grab your fiddle, embrace the tunes, and let the music carry you away on a flight through time and melody.

Applying Bowing Techniques and Fingerings to Play Melodies

Playing the fiddle is like weaving magic through sound, and at the core of this enchanting art form lies the delicate dance between your bow and your fingers. To master the fiddle and create mesmerizing melodies, you must understand how to apply bowing techniques and fingering effectively.

The Bowing Basics

- **The Bow Hold:** Just as a painter wields a brush precisely, a fiddler's path begins with the bow hold. Your thumb and middle finger should gently cradle the frog of the bow while the index and pinky fingers rest lightly on the top. Keep your wrist relaxed and your fingers supple for fluid bowing.

- **Bowing Direction:** The direction of your bowing determines the mood of the music. A simple up or down bow can drastically alter the melody's expression. A down bow is often used for strong, bold notes, while an up bow can add a graceful, airy quality. Practice both to achieve finesse.

14. *The direction of your bowing determines the mood of the music. Source: https://violinspiration.com/wp-content/uploads/down-bow-vs-up-bow-violin-Directions.jpg*

- **Bowing Pressure:** Mastering the right amount of pressure is a delicate art. Too much, and you'll produce a harsh sound. Too little, and the notes may not speak clearly. Experiment to find the sweet spot, bearing in mind that it varies depending on your fiddle's setup and the style of music you're playing.

Fingering the Fiddle

- **Finger Placement:** The placement of your fingers on the fingerboard is crucial to hitting the right notes. For example, to play the note G on the D string, your first finger should gently touch the string while the other fingers remain arched. Each finger covers a different note, creating a musical tapestry.

- **Finger Pressure:** Just as with bowing, finger pressure is critical. Apply too much, and you'll produce a sharp, unpleasant sound. Too little, and the note may not ring out clearly. A gentle, even pressure is key to achieving the desired tone.

- **Finger Vibrato:** Vibrato is the heartbeat of fiddling. It adds warmth and depth to your playing, making your melodies come alive. To master it, practice moving your finger in a slow, controlled rocking motion while maintaining the finger's contact with the string. Gradually increase the speed and width of the motion as you become more comfortable.

Putting It All Together

Now, it's time to see how these bowing techniques and fingerings work harmoniously to play a beautiful fiddle melody. Imagine you're tackling a timeless classic like "Amazing Grace."

1. **Start with Bowing Direction:** Begin with a down bow for the first note to give it a strong, grounded feeling. This note sets the tone for the rest of the melody.

2. **Finger Placement:** Place your fingers precisely on the fingerboard to hit the right notes. In "Amazing Grace," you will play G, A, and B on the D string.

3. **Bowing Pressure:** Apply just the right amount of pressure on the bow. You want the notes to be clear and distinct, with a touch of emotion.

4. **Vibrato for Expression:** As you progress in the melody, use vibrato sparingly to infuse emotion. Perhaps you'll add vibrato to a sustained note, like "saved," to emphasize its significance.

5. **Bowing Variations:** For variation and to keep the melody interesting, try mixing up the bowing direction. Experiment with up bows and down bows in different parts of the song to add dynamics.

6. **Phrasing and Dynamics:** Use your bow and finger control to shape the melody's phrasing and dynamics—crescendo on powerful phrases and diminuendo on softer, more reflective moments.

Remember, mastering the fiddle is a journey of delightful discoveries and constant improvement. Be patient with yourself, practice regularly, and embrace the nuanced interplay between your bow and fingers. As you apply these bowing techniques and fingerings, you'll unlock the true magic of the fiddle, allowing your melodies to soar with grace and emotion.

Reading Basic Sheet Music and Fiddle Tablature

Reading sheet music and tablature opens doors to a treasure trove of melodies and tunes. These notations are the roadmaps guiding you through the musical landscape.

Sheet Music: The Universal Language of Music

Sheet music is a universal notation system used by musicians across genres. It's the blueprint of a musical piece, offering detailed instructions on how to play a melody. Here's how to get started:

15. Sheet music is a universal notation system used by musicians across genres. Source: https://commons.wikimedia.org/wiki/File:Grand_staff_labeled_n otes.svg

1. **The Staff:** The staff consists of five horizontal lines and four spaces, each representing a different note. The lines and spaces represent different pitches, moving from low to high as you ascend.

2. **The Clef:** The treble clef (the G clef) is commonly used in fiddle music. It tells you which notes correspond to the lines and spaces on the staff. For instance, the bottom line of the treble clef staff is E, followed by G, B, D, and F for the other lines above.

3. **Notes:** Notes are the building blocks of sheet music. They appear on the staff as symbols, each representing a specific pitch and duration. A note's position on the staff indicates its pitch, while its shape and the presence of stems and flags determine its duration.

4. **Time Signature:** The time signature, typically at the beginning of a piece, tells you how many beats are in each measure and which note value gets one beat. For example, 4/4 means four beats are in a measure, and a quarter note receives one beat.

5. **Key Signature:** The key signature appears at the beginning of a piece and informs you about the tonal center or key of the music. It dictates which notes are played sharp or flat throughout the piece.

6. **Dynamics and Articulation:** Symbols like crescendos, diminuendos, staccatos, and slurs guide how to express the music with dynamics and articulation.

Fiddle Tablature: Fiddler's Best Friend

Fiddle tablature, or tab, is a notation system tailored specifically for the fiddle and other stringed instruments. It's incredibly useful, especially for those who may not be proficient in reading traditional sheet music.

House of the Rising Sun

16. Fiddle tablature is a notation system tailored specifically for the fiddle and other stringed instruments. Source: https://brentrobitaille.com/wp-content/uploads/2020/07/House-of-the-Rising-Sun-fiddle-tab-violin-tablature.jpg

7. **Strings and Numbers:** The fiddle tablature represents the strings of your instrument, with each line corresponding to a string. The numbers on those lines indicate where the finger should press. For example, "0" means an open string (no fingers

pressing), while "1" corresponds to the first finger, "2" to the second finger, and so on.

8. **Timing:** The horizontal alignment of numbers on each string shows the timing and rhythm. Tabs often use a simple dash or space to represent a short rest or pause between notes.

9. **Slurs and Ties:** Slurs (curved lines connecting notes) and ties (a straight line connecting two notes of the same pitch) indicate phrasing and sustain. It guides you on when to play legato or sustain a note.

10. **Repeats:** Symbols like "||:" and ":||" denote the beginning and end of a repeated section. This helps you recognize patterns in the music.

Bridging the Gap

Now that you understand the basics of sheet music and fiddle tablature, it's time to bridge the gap between the two. Both notations serve the same purpose of guiding you through a piece of music, and they can be used interchangeably.

One valuable exercise is to take a simple tune you're familiar with, whether in sheet music or tablature, and transcribe it into the other format. This exercise reinforces your understanding of both systems.

Learning to read basic sheet music and fiddle tablature is like learning a new language that speaks directly to your fiddler's heart. Whether you prefer the universal language of sheet music or the fiddler's best friend, tablature, both tools empower you to explore and play a rich tapestry of melodies.

Building Fiddle Confidence: Playing Beginner-Friendly Tunes

Embarking on a journey to master the fiddle is like setting sail on a musical adventure. For beginners, it can be both thrilling and challenging. One of the most effective ways to boost your confidence and keep your motivation soaring is by playing beginner-friendly fiddle tunes.

The Power of Beginner-Friendly Tunes

- **Gradual Skill Development:** Like a skyscraper is built brick by brick, your fiddling skills develop one note at a time. Beginner-friendly tunes are designed to introduce you to fundamental techniques, such as fingering, bowing, and basic rhythms, in a manageable way. By mastering these tunes, you build a solid foundation for more complex pieces.

- **Confidence Boost:** Success breeds confidence. When you tackle beginner-friendly tunes and see your progress, no matter how small, you'll feel a surge of accomplishment. This positive feedback loop motivates you to keep practicing and exploring new tunes.

- **Fun and Enjoyment:** Fiddling should be enjoyable from the start. Beginner-friendly tunes often have catchy melodies and straightforward rhythms that make playing them a joyful experience.

Beginner-Friendly Fiddle Tunes to Start with

Here are some fantastic beginner-friendly fiddle tunes that will not only boost your confidence but also bring a smile to your face:

1. "Twinkle, Twinkle, Little Star"

This timeless nursery rhyme is an excellent starting point for beginners. Its melody is simple and familiar, making it easier to focus on mastering your bowing technique and finger placement.

17. This timeless nursery rhyme is an excellent starting point for beginners. Source: https://i.pinimg.com/736x/4e/dc/c8/4edcc8e3d34ae4b0934fd22e0 5c149a3.jpg

2. "Mary Had a Little Lamb"

"Mary Had a Little Lamb" offers a chance to practice transitioning between different notes while maintaining a steady rhythm. It's a stepping stone toward more complex tunes.

3. "BoilThem Cabbage Down"

"Boil Them Cabbage Down" is a traditional fiddle tune that's fun to play and great for building confidence. Its repetitive nature lets you get comfortable with basic fiddle patterns, such as slurs and string crossings.

4. "Skip to My Lou"

"Skip to My Lou" is a folk song with a lively and playful melody. It's perfect for practicing bowing dynamics, adding expression to your playing, and exploring variations in rhythm.

5. "Oh, Susanna"

This American classic offers a taste of fiddling with a touch of storytelling. It introduces you to phrasing and bowing techniques that add character to your playing.

6. "Soldier's Joy" (Simplified Version)

"Solder's Joy" is a well-loved fiddle tune, and there's a simplified version that's beginner-friendly. It allows you to experiment with a bit of speed while keeping the melody relatively simple.

As you journey through these beginner-friendly fiddle tunes, you'll find your confidence steadily growing. Each note you play is a step closer to becoming a skilled fiddler. So, take a deep breath, pick up your fiddle, and let the music carry you on this exciting musical adventure.

Chapter 7: Exploring Fiddle Styles and Techniques

The fiddle's evocative tones have woven their way through the tapestry of countless musical genres, creating a rich and diverse landscape of styles. In this chapter, you'll explore the captivating realm of fiddle playing. You'll discover the distinctive characteristics and techniques of various fiddle styles, from the roots of folk music to the foot-stomping energy of bluegrass.

Whether you're a novice or an experienced fiddler, this chapter will equip you with the knowledge and skills to adapt your playing to different musical genres, opening doors to new and exciting musical possibilities.

Introduction to Various Playing Styles

Before you dive into the intricate details of fiddle styles and techniques, understand that the fiddle is basically a violin. The difference in names is just based on the style of playing. The term "fiddle" is typically associated with folk and traditional music, emphasizing a style of playing that is spirited, improvisational, and deeply rooted in cultural traditions. In contrast, the "violin" is often linked to classical music, featuring a more formal and structured approach.

Folk, Bluegrass, Celtic, and More

Fiddle playing encompasses a wide spectrum of styles, each with unique flavor and heritage. Here are some of the most prominent fiddle styles you'll encounter on your musical journey:

- **Folk Fiddling:** Folk fiddling is the heart and soul of traditional music. It weaves stories of communities, history, and everyday life into its melodies. This style is known for its vibrant, soul-stirring tunes and often includes techniques like slides, drones, and double stops to evoke a sense of time and place.

18. *Folk fiddling is the heart and soul of traditional music. Source: https://www.pexels.com/photo/crop-person-playing-traditional-mongolian-stringed-instrument-in-countryside-4348093/*

- **Bluegrass Fiddling:** Bluegrass fiddling is all about energy and virtuosity. It's the genre that makes you want to tap your foot and dance. Characterized by rapid bowing, intricate ornamentation, and jaw-dropping solos, bluegrass fiddling is a whirlwind of sound that demands precision and passion.

- **Celtic Fiddling:** Transport yourself to the lush green hills of Ireland and Scotland with Celtic fiddling. This style is marked by its hauntingly beautiful airs and lively jigs and reels. Fiddlers use techniques like ornamentation, grace notes, and slurring to capture the essence of Celtic music's rich heritage.

- **Cajun and Zydeco Fiddling:** Heading down to the bayou, you find Cajun and Zydeco fiddling. These lively Louisiana styles infuse elements of French, African, and Creole cultures into their music. Expect infectious rhythms, foot-stomping beats, and a healthy dose of improvisation.

- **Western Swing:** Pioneered by legends like Bob Wills, Western Swing blends country, jazz, and blues into a toe-tapping, swingin' style. Fiddlers in this genre often play with smooth bowing techniques and tasteful improvisation to keep the dance floor rocking.

Learning the Characteristics and Techniques of Each Style

Now that you're familiar with these captivating fiddle styles, it's time to dig deeper into each one and discover the techniques that make them unique.

Folk Fiddling: Embracing Tradition

Folk fiddling is the embodiment of musical storytelling. To master this style, you'll want to focus on the following techniques:

- **Slides:** Sliding notes on the fiddle mimic emotional resonance. Practice sliding smoothly between notes to infuse your playing with depth and feeling.

- **Drones:** Drones are like the steady heartbeat of folk music. Keep a drone note ringing as you play, creating a backdrop that adds a rustic and grounding quality to your tunes.

- **Double Stops:** This is when you play 2 strings at the same time. Experiment with different combinations of double stops to add color to your melodies.

Bluegrass Fiddling: Pickin' with Precision

Bluegrass fiddling is known for its fiery tempo and intricate fingerwork. Here are some key techniques to master:

- **Rapid Bowing:** Speed and precision are the name of the game in bluegrass. Work on your bowing technique to play those lightning-fast runs and keep up with the driving rhythm of the genre.

- **Ornamentation:** Bluegrass fiddlers love to decorate their melodies with slides, slurs, and grace notes. These embellishments add personality and flair to your playing.

- **Double Stops and Crosspicking:** Mastering double stops and crosspicking is essential for creating the layered, textured sound that defines bluegrass. These techniques involve playing multiple strings at once and picking them in intricate patterns.

Celtic Fiddling: Capturing the Spirit

Celtic fiddling transports listeners to a world of mysticism and merriment. To excel in this style, work on the following techniques:

- **Ornamentation Galore:** Celtic fiddlers thrive on ornamentation. Practice adding trills, rolls, and cuts to your melodies to give them that unmistakable Celtic flavor.

- **Grace Notes:** Grace notes are like musical flourishes that add a touch of magic to your tunes. Use them liberally to create a sense of whimsy and whimsicality.

- **Slurring and Bowing Patterns:** Mastering slurring and bowing patterns is key to replicating the lilting, danceable quality of Celtic music. Experiment with different bowing directions and rhythms to bring your melodies to life.

Cajun and Zydeco Fiddling: Get Your Groove on

These Louisiana styles are all about rhythm and groove. Here's what you need to focus on:

- **Syncopation:** Cajun and Zydeco music thrives on syncopated rhythms that make you want to move—practice syncopation in your bowing and left-hand techniques to capture that infectious groove.

- **Accordion Imitation:** Fiddle often imitates the accordion in Cajun and Zydeco music. Work on techniques like drones, rolls, and slides to mimic the accordion's expressive qualities.

- **Swingin' Feel:** These styles have a distinctive swing feel that makes them irresistibly danceable. Experiment with swing bowing patterns and syncopated rhythms to capture that unmistakable Cajun and Zydeco vibe.

Western Swing: Swinging into Style

Western Swing combines the best of country, jazz, and blues.

- **Smooth Bowing:** Western Swing demands smooth, legato bowing. Focus on creating long flowing lines with your bow to achieve that classic Western Swing sound.

- **Jazz Influence:** Jazz elements are prominent in Western Swing, so don't be afraid to explore chromatic scales, improvisation, and swing rhythms to add a jazzy flair to your playing.

19. Jazz elements are prominent in Western Swing. Source: https://pixabay.com/vectors/abstract-jazz-music-melody-notes-7476913/

- **Vocal-like Phrasing:** In Western Swing, fiddlers aim to mimic the human voice. Pay attention to phrasing and dynamics to create melodies that sing and tell a story.

Tips for Adapting to Different Musical Genres

- **Listen Actively:** To excel in any genre, immerse yourself in it. Listen to recordings of the style you want to play. Pay attention to the nuances in tone, rhythm, and ornamentation. The more you listen, the better you'll understand the unique characteristics of the genre.

- **Learn from Masters:** Seek out experienced fiddlers specializing in your chosen genre. Take lessons or attend workshops to learn directly from them. Their guidance and insights can be invaluable in honing your skills.

- **Experiment and Innovate:** While it's essential to respect the traditions of a genre, don't be afraid to add your creative twist. Innovation often leads to the evolution of music, so feel free to experiment with new techniques and ideas while staying true to the essence of the style.

- **Play with Feeling:** No matter the genre, music is a universal language of emotion. Infuse your playing with passion and feeling. Connect with the heart of the music, and your audience will undoubtedly feel it, too.

- **Practice, Practice, Practice:** Lastly, remember that mastering any style takes time and dedication. Practice regularly, work on your technique, and don't be discouraged by challenges. With persistence, you'll unlock the true potential of your fiddle playing.

From the soulful melodies of folk fiddling to the toe-tapping rhythms of bluegrass, each style has its unique charm and demands specific skills. As you continue your musical exploration, remember that versatility is a fiddler's greatest asset. By adapting your playing to different genres, you'll expand your repertoire and enrich your musical experience. So, pick up your fiddle, embrace the diversity of fiddle styles, and let your music resonate with the world.

Chapter 8: Progressing as a Fiddler

Congratulations! You've embarked on a captivating adventure into the world of fiddling, where every note holds a story, and every tune is a window into a rich musical tradition. As you start the final chapter of your fiddling quest, it's essential to reflect on the remarkable progress you've made and look ahead to how you can continue growing as a fiddler. In this chapter, you'll explore strategies to help you set personal goals, grow your techniques, seek guidance, and ultimately become the best fiddler you can be.

Setting Personal Goals and Tracking Your Progress

One of the most powerful tools on your path to fiddling greatness is setting personal goals. Whether you're a beginner or an intermediate player, having clear objectives will guide your practice and ensure you're continually motivated. Here's how to get started:

1. **Define Your Goals:** Ask yourself, "What do I want to achieve as a fiddler?" Your goals could range from mastering a specific tune to performing at a local event. Be specific and realistic when setting your goals. For instance, you might set a short-term goal of learning a particular fiddle tune in the next month and a long-term goal of performing with a local folk band within a year.

2. **Break Goals into Milestones:** Once you've defined your goals, break them into smaller, achievable milestones. This makes your progress more manageable and less overwhelming. If you aim to perform with a local band, your milestones could include learning several tunes and gaining confidence on stage.

3. **Create a Practice Plan:** Now that you have your goals and milestones, create a plan. Dedicate specific times each day or week to practice and be consistent. Practice is the key to improvement in any musical endeavor.

20. Dedicate specific times each day or week to practice and be consistent. Source: https://www.pexels.com/photo/white-paper-with-note-669986/

4. **Track Your Progress:** Keep a journal or use a practice app to record your progress. Note what you've

accomplished, what needs improvement, and any challenges you've faced. Tracking your progress will give you a sense of accomplishment and help you identify areas that need more attention.

Exploring More Advanced Fiddle Techniques and Repertoire

If you've already started your fiddling journey and mastered the basics, it's time to take your skills to the next level. Exploring more advanced fiddle techniques and expanding your repertoire can be both challenging and incredibly rewarding.

Advanced Fiddle Techniques

1. **Double Stops:** As mentioned earlier, this is when you play 2 strings together. While beginners often focus on playing one string at a time, mastering double stops adds depth to your melodies. Start by practicing double stops with scales and simple tunes, gradually incorporating them into more complex pieces. Experiment with different finger combinations to find the tones that resonate most beautifully.

2. **Slides, Hammer-ons, and Pull-offs:** These techniques are the secret ingredients that add flavor and expressiveness to your fiddling.

   - Slides involve smoothly transitioning from one note to another, typically on adjacent strings. Slides can create a seamless connection between notes, adding a touch of elegance to your music.

   - Hammer-ons and pull-offs allow you to articulate notes without re-bowing. A hammer-on is when you use a finger to sound a note on a string without re-bowing, while a pull-off is the opposite, where you release a finger to produce a new note. These techniques are beneficial for creating fast, fluid passages in your tunes.

3. **Bowing Techniques:** Experimenting with bowing patterns and techniques can revolutionize your fiddling style.

- **Staccato:** Play short, detached notes by lifting your bow off the string quickly. This technique is great for adding contrast and rhythm to your playing.

- **Spiccato:** Create a bouncing effect by letting your bow bounce lightly on the strings. Spiccato adds a playful and energetic quality to your music.

- **Tremolo:** Rapidly move your bow back and forth on a single note to create a trembling or shimmering effect. Tremolo is excellent for building tension or emotion in your tunes.

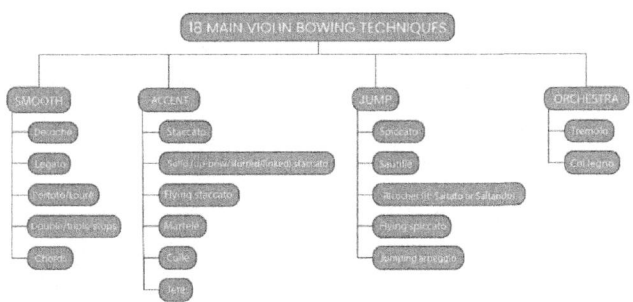

21. *(Note to designer: please remove the word "violin") Experimenting with bowing patterns and techniques can revolutionize your fiddling style. Source: https://violinlounge.com/wp-content/uploads/2022/03/18-MAIN-VIOLIN-BOWING-TECHNIQUES.png*

Expanding Your Repertoire

While mastering advanced techniques is essential, expanding your repertoire is equally important. With a diverse selection of tunes, you get to showcase your versatility as a fiddler and connect with a broader audience.

- **Explore Different Genres:** Don't limit yourself to a single genre of fiddling. Branch out and explore tunes from other musical traditions, such as Celtic, bluegrass, classical, and folk. Each genre brings its singular challenges and flavors, enriching your repertoire.

- **Learn Iconic Pieces:** Consider tackling iconic fiddle pieces that have left a mark in the music world. Classics like "Orange Blossom Special" or "Devil's Dream" are not only fun to play but also serve as great conversation pieces among fellow fiddlers and music enthusiasts.

- **Challenge Yourself:** As you expand your repertoire, don't be afraid to take on challenging tunes. Pushing your boundaries and working on complex pieces will sharpen your skills and make simpler tunes feel more accessible. Remember, growth often occurs outside your comfort zone.

- **Blend Styles:** Get creative by blending different styles within a single tune. Mixing Celtic elements with blues, or classical with folk can result in a unique and captivating musical experience. Let your imagination run wild and see where it takes you.

- **Seek Inspiration:** Listening to a wide range of fiddlers and musicians can inspire new tunes to add to your repertoire. Attend live performances, explore recordings, and immerse yourself in the music to discover hidden gems waiting to be played.

Embrace the challenge of learning double stops, slides, hammer-ons, pull-offs, and other bowing techniques to infuse your music with depth and expressiveness. At the same time, diversify your repertoire by exploring different genres, taking on iconic pieces, and blending styles.

Seeking Guidance from Experienced Fiddlers or Instructors

No fiddler is an island, and seeking guidance from experienced fiddlers or instructors can make a big difference to your progress. Here's how to make the most of mentorship:

- **Find a Mentor:** Look for an experienced fiddler in your local community or online who can give you guidance and feedback. A mentor will help you refine your technique, suggest practice strategies, and share their insights into the art of fiddling.

- **Take Lessons:** Consider enrolling in fiddle lessons with a qualified instructor. Formal instruction will structure your learning and address specific areas that need improvement. Many instructors offer both in-person and online lessons, giving you flexibility in your learning journey.

- **Attend Workshops and Fiddle Camps:** Fiddle workshops and camps are excellent opportunities to learn from multiple experts quickly. These events often feature workshops, jam sessions, and performances, allowing you to immerse yourself in the fiddle community and gain inspiration from fellow fiddlers.

22. Fiddle workshops and camps are excellent opportunities to learn from multiple experts quickly. Source: SylviaStanley, CC BY-SA 4.0 <https://creativecommons.org/licenses/by-sa/4.0>, via Wikimedia Commons: https://commons.wikimedia.org/wiki/File:Shetland_schoolchildre n_fiddlers_age_9-13;_2004.jpg

Tips for Continuous Improvement

- **Embrace Challenges:** Don't shy away from difficult tunes or techniques. Embrace challenges, as they are the stepping stones to growth. Tackling challenging pieces will improve your skills and make simpler tunes seem more accessible.

- **Record Yourself:** Recording your playing is an invaluable practice. It allows you to objectively assess your performance and identify areas for improvement. You can also share your recordings with mentors and peers for feedback.

- **Join a Fiddle Community:** Being part of a fiddle community, whether it's a local jam group or an online forum, can provide a sense of belonging and support. You can exchange ideas, learn new tunes, and find inspiration from other fiddlers.

- **Stay Inspired:** Keep your passion for fiddling alive by staying inspired. Attend concerts, listen to various fiddle styles, and read about the history of the fiddle. Learning about the roots of your music can deepen your connection to it.

As you reach the final notes of this fiddling journey, remember that progress as a fiddler is a continuous and rewarding endeavor. Set clear goals, explore advanced techniques, seek guidance, and follow these improvement tips. Your dedication and love for the fiddle will take you far in this enchanting musical world. So, keep your strings tuned, and let the music flow as you evolve as a fiddler.

Conclusion

In the world of music, learning to play the fiddle is a rewarding journey that opens doors to a rich tradition of melodies and rhythms. In this comprehensive guide, "How to Play the Fiddle for Beginners," you've explored the fundamental aspects of mastering this captivating instrument. As you draw this musical journey to a close, here's a recap of the key takeaways from each chapter and a reflection on the path you've embarked upon.

Key Takeaways

- **Background to the Fiddle:** Understanding the history and significance of the fiddle has given you a deeper appreciation for this versatile instrument. You now know how it has played a crucial role in various musical traditions worldwide.

- **Getting to Know Your Fiddle:** The first step in your fiddling journey was getting acquainted with your instrument. You learned about its parts and how to care for it properly, ensuring it stays in excellent playing condition.

- **Holding and Tuning Your Fiddle:** The correct posture and hand placement are essential for comfortable and practical fiddling. You've mastered holding and tuning your fiddle to produce the best possible sound.

- **Basic Bowing Techniques:** Bowing is the heart and soul of fiddling. You've explored the fundamental bowing techniques, such as the down-bow and up-bow, and how to create beautiful, resonant tones.

- **Learning Essential Fiddle Fingerings:** Fingering techniques are crucial for hitting the right notes. You've delved into the finger positions for different scales, ensuring you can play accurately and melodically.

- **Playing Your First Fiddle Tunes:** You've reached an exciting milestone by learning to play your first fiddle tunes. From "Twinkle, Twinkle, Little Star" to folk classics, you've built a repertoire of delightful melodies.

- **Exploring Fiddle Styles and Techniques:** This book has introduced you to a world of fiddle styles, from Celtic to bluegrass, and techniques like double stops and vibrato. These skills have expanded your musical horizons.

- **Progressing as a Fiddler:** Your journey doesn't end here. You've gained the knowledge and confidence to continue developing your fiddling skills. With practice, dedication, and a love for music, you can become a skilled fiddler.

As you embark on your fiddling journey, remember that progress takes time and patience. Each practice session brings you closer to mastering this beautiful instrument. Share your music with friends and family, and perhaps even consider joining a local jam session or fiddling community to enhance your skills.

Please take a moment to leave a review, sharing your thoughts and experiences with "How to Play the Fiddle for Beginners." Your input will help improve and inspire future fiddlers on their musical quests.

The fiddle holds a world of melodies and emotions waiting to be explored. May your fiddling journey be filled with joy, creativity, and the sheer delight of making music. Thank you for choosing this book as your guide, and may your fiddle always sing sweetly in your hands.

References

Basic techniques - Learn fiddle technique. (2014, April 30). Fiddle Lessons. and Workshops; Edinburgh fiddle workshops. https://www.fiddleclass.com/basic-techniques/

Hart, K. (n.d.). Musical playgrounds: All about fiddling. AAA State of Play. https://www.aaastateofplay.com/musical-playgrounds-all-about-fiddling/

History of fiddle. (2021, February 15). Georgia Pick and Bow Traditional Music School. https://www.georgiapickandbow.org/history-of-fiddle/

How to play A fiddle. (2013, February 28). Lessonface. https://www.lessonface.com/content/how-play-fiddle

Sugar, A. (2023a, February 15). How to learn fiddle tunes by ear: And why you should learn. Takelessons.com. https://takelessons.com/blog/how-to-learn-fiddle-tunes-by-ear-and-why-you-should-learn

Sugar, A. (2023b, June 20). An introduction to the world of fiddle tunes. Takelessons.com. https://takelessons.com/blog/an-introduction-to-the-world-of-fiddle-tunes

The Editors of Encyclopedia Britannica. (2019). fiddle. In Encyclopedia Britannica.

TNM. (2022, May 7). How to Play Fiddle in 14 Days. Troy Nelson Music | Music Lesson Books and Songbooks. https://troynelsonmusic.com/how-to-play-fiddle-in-14-days/

Wise, O. (2022, June 23). Listen to the past: 7 tips on learning old-time fiddle. Strings Magazine. https://stringsmagazine.com/7-tips-on-learning-old-time-fiddle/

Printed in Dunstable, United Kingdom

67628176R00057